MW01169723

Bold Moves To Creating Financial Wealth™

Bold Moves To Creating Financial Wealth™

by

GERALD GRANT JR. MBA

G & G ENTERPRISES OF MIAMI, INC.

Published by:
G & G ENTERPRISES OF MIAMI, INC.
P.O. Box 566567
Miami, FL 33256-6567
(786) 459-8282

ISBN Hardcover: 978-0-9826453-0-7
ISBN Paperback: 978-0-9826453-1-4

Library of Congress Control Number: 2010901971

Printed in the United States of America

Contents

List of Tables and Charts

Acknowledgements

THE first people I want to thank are my panel of advisors who guided me along the way as I wrote this book: Marc Henderson, author Robert Roots, Kervin Clenance, Connie Crowther, Marlon Hill, and Jerome Hutchinson.

I must also thank Rochelle Adger, my sister-in-law, Winsome Cox, Jasmin Grant, Donovan Terrelonge, James Bussey, Ivelaw Griffith, Jesse Tyson and Willis Greene for their outstanding efforts and support as they assisted with numerous drafts of editing, proofing and rewriting of this book. Without their assistance, I could not have done it.

Special thanks to my sister-in-law Cheryl Fields and Medium Four Marketing Energy + Design Company for designing the book cover. I would also like to thank my extended family at Sweet Home Missionary Baptist Church in Miami, Florida for their support and encouragement to complete this book.

Most of all I want to thank my best friend and wife Jennifer, my daughter Jasmin, and my son Gerald III, for their patience, love, and continuous support as I wrote this book.

This book is dedicated to all
who are committed to taking the
Bold Moves to Creating Financial Wealth

It's your move...

Introduction

CREATING WEALTH: HOW DO YOU GET THERE FROM HERE AND KEEP IT?

MY twenty-five years of career experience as a banker and financial professional, along with my childhood experiences, have uniquely prepared me with a wealth of experience. Studying for my professional designation exams provided me with information about budgeting, debt management, buying cars, buying homes, purchasing life insurance, college funding, retirement planning, investing, income taxes, and wills and trusts.

My dad taught me one of the most important principles of business. I grew up in Jamaica, where my dad was a shoemaker. I noticed how he would observe his employees taking care of clients, and if there was a situation that they could not resolve, he would step in and say, "no problem." He believed in the concept that the client was always right, and he would do whatever it took to resolve the problem. That experience taught me how a business should be run. Without serving my clients, I have no business. If I give my clients what they want, they give me what I want. This experience has helped me see things through the eyes of my clients and has helped me tremendously to be successful in business.

My former career as a banker has placed me in a position to impact the lives of many people. Early in my career, I discovered that it was necessary to take the time needed to educate clients about the advantages and features of the products offered by the bank. We educated new clients on how to use their debit cards, and it made their banking more convenient. It was easier for them to use their debit cards to get cash at the ATMs instead of waiting in a long line to cash a small check. It was easier for them to use their debit cards to pay for groceries or to purchase gas instead of using cash. It was also safer to use their debit cards to make those purchases instead of walking around with large sums of cash. This educational process also applied to other areas, such as helping first-time homebuyers qualify for buying their homes, and showing clients how to improve their credit scores so they could qualify for credit cards and automobile loans.

I realized that educating clients was a critical component of helping them meet their goals. I started having monthly seminars on a variety of subjects, ranging from investments, to income tax management, to wills and trusts. The clients were pleased with the information they received and were encouraged to bring their family and friends to upcoming seminars. After these forums, a number of clients would approach me to get my opinion, instead of the advisors who had made the presentations. Because I had developed a good relationship with them, they wanted me to tell them what to do. Little did I know that these presentations were preparing me for my career as a financial professional.

My role as a financial professional has been a true joy. I see myself more as a financial doctor. Clients have different goals and aspirations, and I help them quantify their objectives, prepare a financial game plan, and develop time frames around them. Most people have an idea of what they want, but they don't know how to achieve it. When medical doctors have new clients, they ask them to complete a number of questions to get their medical history. Their doctors want to know if they have any existing or previous medical conditions, or if they are allergic to certain medications. Doctors usually begin with this question:

"What is the specific reason for your appointment?" By gathering this information they are able to better understand your needs. Your doctor may have you complete a number of tests and will analyze the results. Upon reviewing the results he or she may write a prescription to help you achieve the desired medical solution. Your doctor would schedule a follow-up appointment to see if the prescription was effective in improving your health. If the first prescription didn't work, your doctor may prescribe another medication. This process is very similar to working with a financial professional. To understand your goals, financial professionals normally ask questions to determine your financial health and offer recommendations to help you achieve your desired financial strategy. Just like medical doctors, they will need to monitor your financial prescription to make sure it is working properly, and if the desired results are not being achieved, they'll discuss additional recommendations.

Unfortunately, financial literacy is seldom taught in high school or college—it's something people are expected to learn on their own. The truth is you can have a master's degree and still not understand how to manage money. Many of my clients are professionals who run large organizations and create tremendous incomes, but they have not fully mastered all aspects of managing money. This book will teach you how to create and transfer wealth. Many of the concepts I will share in this book are not new; however, the execution of them is unique. I want to share this information in a way that will get you to do something about your finances now. One of my passions in life is to educate as many people as possible about how they can take control of their financial lives.

In 1987, I attended a conference in Los Angeles, where Dr. Marty Cohen was the motivational speaker. It is amazing, when you are in the right place at the right time, how things can impact your life. The two hours shared with Dr. Cohen changed my life. He explained that the information he was sharing were the tools to help us improve our lives, but unfortunately, only a small percentage of the people listening to him would use those tools.

We all have good intentions, but few people will take action immediately and implement new ideas. I was one of those few. Following that conference, I committed to implementing his ideas. My commitment resulted in me achieving the "Manager of the Year" for Great Western Bank in Florida for two successive years. My desire for you is that the information in this book will make a significant impact on your life and motivate you to take the actions necessary to change your life.

Today is the first day of your new lifestyle. It doesn't matter what you've done so far. It only matters what you will do to live the life you've dreamed about. Overcoming financial illiteracy is very similar to someone wanting to learn how to lose weight. Just imagine walking into the gym for the first time, seeing all the different equipment, and not understanding how to use them. If the equipment isn't used properly, instead of helping you, they can hurt you. What you would need is a personal trainer, and you don't have to be a millionaire to hire one.

The personal trainer will start by asking you what you want to accomplish. He or she will take your measurements to find out where you are, and then create a plan to help you accomplish your goals. This is also true for financial professionals. You don't have to be a millionaire to have a financial professional. All you need is the desire to improve your finances, and the professional can help you create a plan toward achieving your goals. The secret to achieving your financial goals is establishing and executing your plan.

I am writing this book about creating and transferring wealth from three points of view:

- If you don't have it, how do you get it?
- If you have it, how do you make it better?
- If you made it better, how do you keep it in the family?

CHAPTER 1

What Are The Bold Moves to Financial Independence?

To get there from here, you must know where "there" is. To make sure we are on the same page, let's review Webster's definitions of "create" and "wealth."

> create: (1) to cause to come into being, as something unique, (2) to evolve from one's imagination as a work of art or invention, (3) To perform (a role) in the production of a play or motion picture, (4) to make by investing with, (5) to arrange or bring out by intention or design

> wealth: (1) a great quantity or store of money, property or other riches, (2) plentiful amount: abundance.

Just as Webster's definitions of "create" and "wealth" have different meanings, people take different routes in the creation of wealth. Some people want it right away; this is why so many states have a lottery. Everyone wants to win, but there are only a few winners. Some people gamble at casinos and may win in the short run, but in the long run, only the casino owners are the winners. They wouldn't be in business if most of their clients won all the time. Some people achieve wealth by being professional athletes. If you calculate how many high school athletes become professional athletes, the percentage is very small. If you also calculate the number of professional athletes who are still in the business after four years, the number is even smaller. Some people acquire their wealth by inheritance. Others earn it the old-fashioned way, by working all their lives to build a business. Regardless of how they get there, they need discipline and the understanding of money management to stay there. Regardless of who you are, you can spend money faster than the time it takes to make it. Creating wealth isn't just about making money; creating wealth is about managing and maintaining it so that you can have peace of mind and enjoy it for a lifetime.

Your journey should start with the end in mind; "What are the Bold Moves to financial independence?" I'll answer this with a story. I met a police officer who was considering retiring at age 62. After gathering all his information and completing my analysis, the results were that this officer was eligible for retirement, but wasn't financially able to retire. I could see the disappointment in his face, and his response was, "Where were you when I started working at age 22?" I could hear the pain in his voice. Step into his shoes for a moment. If you were age 62 and couldn't retire, what would you do differently? I showed him how to reduce his living expenses and created additional income during retirement by doing something he liked. For him, this was the right adjustment that made his retirement enjoyable.

Travel with me on a journey of the life of someone who has accumulated wealth and was pleased with the results, and then compare your financial literacy to where you are on the path.

The common timeline for students is that most of them graduate from high school by the age of 18. Wouldn't it be great to have a timeline that would lead towards financial independence on or before age 65?

Take a few moments to look at the charts located on the next two pages.

Timeline of the Bold Moves

| Early Education Through High School | Post High School Education | Post College Education |

WEALTHY INDIVIDUALS

1. Go to school 2. Learn to save 3. Graduate from high school	1. Start working 2. Establish credit 3. Buy cars 4. Get first apartment 5. Learn how to manage money 6. Go to college 7. Start investing	1. Graduate from college 2. Get married 3. Buy a house 4. Have children 5. Buy life insurance 6. Start retirement planning 7. Buy disability insurance 8. Start college funding for children 9. Establish wills

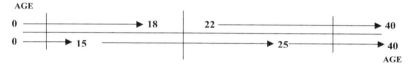

AGE

0 ——————→ 18   22 ——————→ 40

0 ——→ 15 ——————→ 25 ——→ 40

AGE

NON-WEALTHY INDIVIDUALS

1. Go to school	1. Start working 2. Establish credit 3. Buy cars 4. Get first apartment	1. Get married 2. Have children 3. Buy a house 4. Start retirement planning

Timeline of the Bold Moves

Mid-life Career Education	Retirement Education

WEALTHY INDIVIDUALS

1. Make wise investments after seeking advice
2. Start their own business
3. Children graduate from college
4. Buy cars for children
5. Buy homes for children
6. Teach children to invest

1. Start retirement
2. Buy LTC (Long Term Care)
3. Start college funding for grandchildren
4. Take care of parents
5. Establish trust for children and grandchildren
6. Teach grandchildren to invest

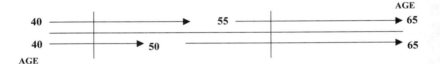

NON-WEALTHY INDIVIDUALS

1. Make unwise investments without seeking advice
   EXAMPLES:
   - Starting a business without doing the research.
   - Buying investments based on tips received from individuals who are not experts.
2. Buy life insurance in smaller amounts
3. Buy disability insurance
4. Help their children pay for college

1. Start retirement
2. Start college funding for grandchildren
3. Take care of parents
4. Establish wills

The chart shows that wealth-creating individuals form habits that most people don't follow. Most kids go to school; however, the children of wealthy parents are expected to develop habits such as learning how to save money. They are expected to graduate from high school, and then go to college. College is an opportunity to develop your skills, to have a career that will provide for the well-being of you and your family.

Children who don't complete high school have severely limited their career choices, resulting in low paying jobs. They start working at an early age. Due to lack of resources, they try to establish credit to buy the things that they need. Instead of buying houses, they rent apartments. On the other hand, children of wealth-creating parents are expected to go to college and continue building their savings. As their savings accumulate, they start to learn how to invest in the stock market.

Between the ages of 22 and 40, kids who don't go to college get married; they then have children and finally start their retirement planning. While children who go to college are doing the same thing, a major difference is that upon graduation, these children get higher-paying jobs and can buy homes at an earlier age. They purchase life insurance to protect their families. They also buy disability insurance to protect their income if they are injured in an accident. These children reap the benefits of a college education and save for their children's college education. In many instances, they also prepare wills and trusts for their families in case of their premature death.

Between ages 40 to 55, individuals who didn't go to college try to make up the income gap by starting a business. In many cases, their business fails, due to either poor planning or lack of financial resources to make it through the first two years. Sometimes they buy investments based on tips received from individuals who aren't experts. Most of these investments don't live up to expectations because they were bought on hunches instead of choices made after research and careful consideration.

At the same ages, individuals who are entrepreneurial start their own businesses. Some of these successful entrepreneurs hire their children when they graduate from college and help them purchase cars and homes. If their children have not mastered investing, they spend time teaching them how to develop this skill.

At ages 50 and older, the non-wealthy individuals approach retirement and realize that they are not prepared to retire. In some cases, they may be eligible to retire, but financially, they can't stop working. In many cases, because they are eligible, they do retire only to discover that they must go back to work to maintain their quality of life or to help their children or parents. On the other hand, individuals with wealth can maintain their quality of life during retirement, provide college funding for their grandchildren, and take care of parents if necessary. To ensure their wealth is transferred to the next generation, they prepare wills and trusts to maximize the funds retained within the family. To reduce the size of their taxable estate, wealthy clients establish trusts for their family members and teach the grandchildren how to invest.

How Do You Get There From Here?

Regardless of where you fall in this timeline, the decisions you make today will impact the rest of your life. You can use this opportunity to improve your situation, and you can also use this time to help others benefit from your experience or lack of experience. It doesn't matter how much money you make, but it does matter how you manage it.

Let's stop and evaluate where you are now. Are you where you want to be? Do you have the peace of mind that you desire?

Where you are, right now, is our starting point of your journey to financial freedom. To help you get where you want to be, we must first know where you are. For many people, this is a wake-up call. They know they want something different, but they never stop to get their bearings. We are all at different points on our journeys. We cannot change the past, but we have full control over what we can do to impact our future. Today, we begin your journey.

Creating wealth is relative to each person. Each of us has our own reasons why we create wealth. For some people, being wealthy means being able to provide for their family and live a modest life during retirement. For others, it means being able to provide college funding for their children so they can have a better financial future. Some people want luxury homes, fancy cars, big yachts, and the financial freedom to travel around the world. Others want to expand a successful business to multiple locations.

Even though people have different reasons for wanting wealth, the one thing they all have in common is desire. To be successful at anything requires a lot of effort and persistence. You have spent your entire life creating the habits that govern the things you do today. It will take some time to change those habits into new ones. Some of the biggest differences in life are made by some of the smallest changes that we make. Let's make a big change towards your financial independence.

What are your reasons for making the Bold Moves? Take a moment and write them down. They will be the drivers that will aid you in achieving your goals. My vision is to partner with you on your journey to financial freedom. Everything we do together starts in your mind. If you don't believe it, then you will never achieve it.

A good place to start your financial freedom is to build a great foundation. This leads us to our next chapter that explains how to create your ideal budget.

Summary

- Evaluate where you are now.
- Understand your reasons for making a change.
- Understand that it takes a lot of effort to change.
- List your reasons for making the Bold Moves.

CHAPTER 2

Your Ideal Budget

WHEN most people hear the word, "budget," they cringe. To them, this word has negative connotations. When people think of budgets, they think of control. Most people don't like being told what to do and when to do it. Sometimes they get an attitude, as in, "I'm going to decide what to do with my money, and it's none of your business." My goal today is to get you to think about the word, "budget," differently. Instead of focusing on the word, "budget," I want you to think about the way you live your life. All successful companies have a budget. If it works for the most successful companies, isn't it a possibility that it could work for you? Let's examine budgeting from the following points of view:

- The purpose of budgeting
- Formulating the ideal budget
- What should be included in your ideal budget?
- A simple tracking system for expenses
- Saving for quarterly and annual expenses
- Saving for your wish list

THE PURPOSE OF BUDGETING

The purpose of budgeting is to help you increase your awareness of your spending habits. By increasing your awareness, you will maximize all your resources. A number of my clients have shared with me that they're not sure where their money is going. They know that they get a paycheck, and they know that they pay their bills. However, they feel they have little control over what's left over at the end of the month. This can be discouraging because it appears that there's no light at the end of the tunnel. A budget lets you see the light.

FORMULATING THE IDEAL BUDGET

Many people have never used a budget, so how do you formulate one? It's easy. Start with the things you do on a regular basis. The easiest and the most impressive budget plan I have seen was one used by one of my senior citizen clients. It was clear to me why she was financially independent. Before her husband passed away, he showed her how to list each transaction on a note pad when she spent money. The expenses listed on each page were by month. Also included was the income received for that month. The client was able to see, on a monthly basis, her expenses and income. She realized over time that her expenses were increasing and made sure her investment portfolio grew to keep up with her living expenses. The truly impressive part of this process is that she had been doing this for over twenty years, and she had kept all the journals from the time she started. That was incredible.

What Should Be Included in the Ideal Budget?

The following should be considered when creating your ideal budget:

- The expenses of all family members
- Monthly income sources
- Cash flow differences
- A simple tracking system for expenses
- Savings for quarterly or annual expenses
- Family wish list

It is important to take into account the needs of all family members when establishing the ideal budget. One key area often overlooked is purchasing for children and grandchildren. Parents and grandparents may limit the amount of money they spend on themselves, but they go overboard and don't limit the funds spent on children's activities. Children and grandchildren are members of the family and there should be a line item in the budget to control these expenditures.

Another key area that should be a line item in the budget is expenses for gifts or contributions to help other family members. I have seen too often that it's hard for a number of clients to say no when it comes to helping family members, and they end up jeopardizing their own financial stability by overextending this assistance. These clients sometimes don't realize that their family members won't stop asking, as long as the help keeps coming. You should not give to family members more than you can afford to lose. Family members, in most cases, intend to pay you back, but if they're having financial difficulties, they may not be able to return the funds. By limiting your contribution to gifts instead of loans, you will have no hard feelings if the funds are never paid back.

When establishing a budget, most people only think about expenses; however, a budget should include both expenses and income. Income includes money from all sources, such as salary, rents, social security, pension, investments, and trusts. When income comes from salary, I normally suggest that the client include only the base income. Sometimes clients include overtime income as if it were part of their base pay, increasing their level of spending to match their take-home pay, only to find difficulties when the overtime income stops.

When recording your income, you should consider when the funds are received. For example, some people get paid every two weeks; others get paid on a monthly basis. It is important to include the dates when your income is received, because in real life, your expenses don't always match these dates. You must save income for periods when it doesn't match your expenses. Some people are paid by commissions and their income varies from paycheck to paycheck. If this is your situation, it would be best to take an average of the monthly income instead of using the lowest or highest check amount. The average income is a more realistic indication of income for someone who works on a commission basis.

A Simple Tracking System for Expenses

Many of my clients started out keeping track of the money they spent on a daily basis by listing it on a note pad. They began very encouraged, but soon, the details of writing every transaction became boring. They sometimes forgot to list some of the transactions and didn't always remember how all the money was spent. This process is sometimes frustrating for a number of clients, but there is a way to avoid this frustration.

What's the best way to collect this information now that you are aware of the income and expenses for the ideal budget? I recommend to my clients that they spend as little cash as possible, and let the bank and credit card companies capture this information for them. When you write checks, this information is captured on your bank statement and checkbook register. When you use your credit card, this information is captured on your monthly credit card statement. It is easier to retrieve this information from your checking account and credit card statements than it is to try to list the transactions on a legal pad.

For individuals who are not computer-savvy, an easy way to capture the monthly expenses is to list the transactions from credit card statements and the checkbook register for one year on a twelve-column accounting pad. In the first column, list the type of expenses. In the adjacent columns, fill in the corresponding dollar amounts for each month (January – December). Total each column and divide by 12 to get your monthly average. Capturing this information for an entire year allows you to see your spending patterns throughout the year.

Sample of Annual or Monthly Expenses (Dollars)					
Description	Jan	Feb	March...	Total	Monthly Averages
Car Payment	400	400	400	4,800	400
Charitable Contributions	400	350	450	4,800	400
Grocery	750	850	800	9,600	800
Cash	400	350	450	4,800	400
Dining Out	250	150	200	2,400	200
Movies	50	25	75	600	50
Telephone/Cell/Internet	200	250	300	3,000	250

These numbers become your starting point towards formulating your ideal budget. Don't get discouraged with this process. The main purpose of this exercise is to increase your awareness of how you're spending money. As you continue this practice, you will see a pattern of the expenses that you pay on a monthly basis.

You are already aware of your routine expenses. We're trying to find the areas where you are spending money but you aren't aware of how much you are spending. If you pay your mortgage payment every month, you know what the monthly payment is. However, I'm more concerned about the electric bill, for example. For some people, during the summer months, these bills are extremely high. For others, this expense is higher in the winter months. It is necessary to put reserves away for the higher expenses during these periods, to avoid a financial hardship. Capturing information at this detail level isn't easy, but the increased level of awareness is worth the effort.

I encourage all my married clients to sit down jointly to do this process. This joint exercise can become a real eye-opener for individual spending. If you aren't the person going to the grocery store on a weekly basis, then you probably don't know how much food really costs. It's very important that the information you record is as accurate as possible, so before starting this process, I normally say to each client, "If you get upset when you learn the information, then your spouse/significant other isn't going to share it with you." For most of my clients, the biggest surprises are in the areas of dining out, clothing, vacations, kid's activities, emergencies, and gifts. These can create cash flow problems if they aren't monitored properly.

SAVING FOR QUARTERLY AND ANNUAL EXPENSES

One key component of the ideal budget is saving for emergencies. A general rule of thumb: If there is only one income earner or one source of income, your emergency fund should be six times your monthly expenses. On the other hand, if there are two income earners or more than one source of income, then the emergency fund should be three times your monthly expenses. This reinforces the importance of knowing how much your monthly expenses are. This is the foundation of ensuring that you set aside adequate funds so that you can cover common quarterly and annual expenses—not if they occur, but when they occur.

For example, let's say you bought a set of tires for your car 24 months ago. You took your car in for a regular service and learned that you needed to replace the tires. That's when it hits you: every 24 months you'll need new tires. This will be an annual expense that you can prepare for. You'll need to divide the price that you paid for the tires by 24, and set aside those funds on a monthly basis, so that they will accumulate in your savings and be available to fund your next set of tires. This concept is the same for any expense that isn't paid on a monthly basis that will occur within one year. Examples include the following: homeowner's insurance and property taxes, (if they're not held in an escrow account with your mortgage), or funds for vacation, gifts, and contributions to assist other family members.

Saving For Your Wish List

Sometimes the things people want are overlooked. Each family member should have a wish list, three things that he or she really wants, according to the priority of what is most important. As additional resources become available, these items can be purchased. For example, you may want to replace that old TV that isn't working properly, or it may be time to get a new car for the family, or that beautiful suit that your significant other has always wanted. The wish list takes away the impulse buying that television commercials create. It also discourages the impulse buying associated with shopping at the mall.

The importance of having a wish list is that it encourages you to buy what each family member really wants. It also becomes a tool to limit what items are purchased. If someone wants to buy something and it's not on the wish list, the answer is simple: no. Anyone who wants something new will need to evaluate the importance of the new item and either replace it with something already on the list or add it to the list. This way, you are all making a conscious decision about your purchases.

Now that you have an idea of your living expenses, we will identify large expenses and ways to lower those cost in our next chapter.

Summary

- Increase your awareness of how you are spending money.
- Include income, spending, and savings in your ideal budget.
- Follow the steps to formulate the ideal budget.
- Follow a simple tracking system for expenses.
- Save for quarterly and annual expenses.
- Create a wish list for each family member.

CHAPTER 3

Identifying Large Living Expenses And Lowering Costs in Unique Ways

Eating Out

LET'S review some of these surprise areas in more detail. For a number of clients, a large portion of their income is spent on dining out. Not until they start tracking their expenditures do they realize how much money they are really spending in this area. Dining out at restaurants is so much more convenient than preparing meals at home that it's easy to see why people do it. But when you start to add up the cost of eating out during the week, including the amount of money spent for lunches, you discover how easily it can get out of control. With a little planning, you can greatly reduce these expenses.

One way to control them is to set a dollar amount for eating out and stay within your budget. For example, instead of buying sandwiches for lunch at the local deli, it may be more cost-effective to take a sandwich to work. Another way to save money is to cook multiple meals on Sunday for the remainder of the week. Instead of cooking just one meal, you can put something in the oven that will be the meals for Monday and Wednesday, while preparing something else on the stovetop for Tuesday and Thursday. Prepare another meal on the grill for Sunday while you are putting the prepared meals for Monday through Thursday in the refrigerator. This plan has been effective for a number of working parents who don't have time during the week to prepare meals.

Grocery Shopping

The savings gained by preparing meals for the entire week can be lost in how you shop for the food. A general rule of thumb is to never go to the grocery store when you're hungry. Because your appetite is strong, you will purchase a considerable number of unnecessary items, thus increasing your spending. To ensure that you keep this in control, prepare a list before going shopping for groceries. A number of people review the Sunday paper for coupons that can result in big savings at the grocery store.

Another way to lower your food costs is by bending down two feet. Merchants increase their profits by placing their most expensive products at eye level. In many instances, the manufacturers of the most popular brands also prepare the store brands that are found on the lower shelves. Try this experiment: The next time you go shopping for your favorite brand, also buy the store brands. Prepare both brands at the same time. If you can't taste the difference, you've just discovered an excellent discount by buying the store brand. Finally, when you think you're done, and you're about to leave the store, watch out at the checkout line. While waiting to pay for your groceries, you'll find catchy things like magazines, candy, soda, and bottled water. These are the most profitable items in the store; resist buying them.

Several clients have also discovered that shopping at warehouse stores, such as BJ's and Costco, is another way to reduce their grocery costs. For individuals with families, this can be effective in lowering the grocery bills. Purchasing items such as cleaning supplies, soaps, paper towel and tooth paste in bulk can lead to significant savings over time.

Retail Shopping

As I speak around the country, the most popular subject for my audience is my sharing how they can save 20 to 50 percent shopping for clothing. Everyone wants to know how to do it, so here's how.

Most people don't know that there is a sale at their favorite retail stores every 30 days that isn't advertised. I discovered the secret while working for a major retail store nearly 30 years ago. Two major reasons why merchandise prices are reduced occur almost every month. One reason goods are marked down is the lack of space, and another is that buyers for the stores may not have funds available in their budget to pay for the merchandise they want.

Lowering costs motivate shoppers to make more purchases, in turn providing additional space for merchandise. How can you use this to your advantage? Many retail stores have commissioned salespeople, and by establishing a relationship with them, you can create your own personal shoppers. Have you ever noticed how well-dressed retail salespeople are? The reason is that they are the first to hear about these sales, called markdowns. Approximately every 30 days there is a major sales event—major holidays or Mothers Day or Father's Day, for example. Stores may purchase the merchandise for these special events six to nine months in advance, scheduling its delivery around six to eight weeks before an event.

This is a problem for retail stores because they have limited storage space, which creates the opportunity for you. To create space, stores mark merchandise down so that it can be sold quickly to make room for new merchandise.

Many shoppers have problems finding their size when there

is a big sale. This is where the commissioned salespeople can help you. The next time you go shopping, instead of just window-shopping, identify the items you want. List the items on the back of a business card, along with your size. If you don't have a business card, you can go to your local stationery store and have 500 cards printed with your name and phone number for about $10. Give your business card to the salespeople, who are now your "personal shoppers," and have her or him call you when the merchandise is marked down. Just imagine the great feeling of walking into a store and having that jacket or pant in your size and on sale, waiting for you. This gives you the opportunity to buy something that you wouldn't normally buy because it's above your price range, but because its price is now 50 percent lower, it fits into your budget.

The secret to making this process work is that when the personal shoppers call you they are expecting you to come in and buy something. If you don't come, they may not call you the next time or possibly remove your card from their list. Because they're commissioned salespeople, the process creates a win-win situation for you and the salesperson. My family has enjoyed this benefit for the past 30 years, and we have developed great relationships with many commissioned salespeople. The shopping experience is so much better when you can select from a number of items, they're all at the right price, and they're all items you want. It's a lot more fun when you're shopping and all the items are 50 percent off.

TRAVEL

Another area of potential savings is vacation travel. In today's fast-moving world, many people feel it is less costly to purchase their own travel ticket or make their own arrangements via the Internet, instead of working with a travel agent. In some cases this is true, but in the long run, working with a travel agent can enhance your vacation experience. The insight from a travel agent can make your trip more enjoyable and also save you time and money. For example, travel agents sometimes work with the airline and hotel industries to develop promotional packages. By combining the savings on the airline ticket with the discount of the hotel room, a trip that was outside your budget is now possible.

A number of clients have shared with me that they haven't been able to afford to take a vacation. On the other hand, I've shared with them that they cannot afford not to take a vacation. This is the choice: A person can either spend the money on a vacation or spend more money for medicine. I can assure you it is more fun to spend the money on a vacation than it is to spend for medicine because you become sick from working too much. For many people who don't take vacations, the stress of day-to-day job details eventually makes them sick.

After a relaxing vacation, it's amazing how ready you are to face the problems that had you so stressed out. Sometimes you need rest and relaxation to get reenergized, and that allows you to deal with problems much differently. Paying the extra cost for a travel agent is often worth the price, considering the benefit that comes from their experience. Instead of just getting a cheap room, you get a room with a view and can enjoy a beautiful sunset. Instead of just saving money on a hotel room located on the wrong side of the city, you can get the right room, from which you can enjoy shopping and dining within walking distance of the hotel. You might have saved on the hotel room, but if, in the long run, you spent more for taxis and dining out and had less quality time with your family, then you actually lost. Until you experience the difference a travel agent can make, you will never realize how important they are.

Now that you have learned how to lower larger expenses, it's time to move to the next chapter to look at the details of establishing a budget.

Summary

- Lower eating costs by cooking multiple meals at the same time.
- Never shop when you are hungry and take a shopping list to the store.
- Buy merchandise that is on sale and use a personal shopper.
- Use a travel agent for major trips.

CHAPTER 4

Establishing a Budget

NOW that we've identified all the items that should be included in the budget, let's talk about how to establish a budget. The first line item on your budget should be paying yourself. You pay your telephone bill, you pay your electric bill, and you pay your rent or mortgage company. Many of my clients who are Christians believe in tithing; they contribute the first tenth of their earnings to their church. The same discipline that is used in tithing can be used in paying yourself.

Most people do it the other way around. After they pay their bills, they apply what's left over to savings. Unfortunately, most of the time, there is nothing left to save. We must learn to put ourselves first. We must learn that if we want to save we have to take control of that process. I suggest that if saving is not at the top of your priorities, it should be very close to it. Let's take a closer look at the sample budget in the chart on pages 42 & 43.

When I started using this form many years ago, it had about eleven lines. This form was first used when I did credit counseling, and it was a good starting point for the clients to see how they were spending their money. To make this process real for them, I wanted them to add to this budget any expense that was unique to their family situation and not on the form. Over the years, the number of lines continued to grow considerably. It became necessary to start grouping the expenses by category. For example, if someone was considering moving from a smaller home to a larger home, the expenses that would be important at this time would be the housing expenses. By listing the expenses before the move and the projected expenses after the move, the client could see if they could afford to make the move on paper before actually moving.

Unfortunately, a lot of people didn't do this exercise until after they had moved. That's when they realized that the property taxes and the electric bill would be higher because the home was larger. They were suddenly financially stretched. Bigger is not always better if you can't afford it. Listing the expenses by category is only the first step.

Keep in mind a few points about using this form. To identify your disposable income, be careful not to include items twice. For example, don't list property taxes and homeowner's insurance as expense items if they are included in your mortgage payment. This point also applies to deductions from your paycheck such as: retirement savings, car loans, personal savings, or medical, life, disability, and long-term care insurance. If you list these deductions as expenses, remember to add them back to your net pay as a part of your disposable income. Another way to handle these expenses is not to list them because they are captured on your pay stub and have already been deducted from your disposable income.

Another area where information may be counted twice is credit card purchases. If you pay your entire credit card balance on a monthly basis, these items should be listed in categories based on how the funds were spent such as: gas, vacations, gifts, or entertainment. This information is helpful because it increases your awareness of how you are spending your funds. The credit card payment category is reserved for those cards where you have a balance and you are making monthly payments.

Sample Budget

Client Name: John and Susan Johnson

	Monthly	Annual	Annualized Expense
Personal Savings			
5%			-
10%	800		9,600
20%			-
Total	800	-	9,600
Charitable Contributions			
House of Worship	800		9,600
Other			-
Total	800	-	9,600
Housing			
Mortgage/Rent	1,000		12,000
Community Dues	100		1,200
Electricity/Gas & Water	250		3,000
Water			-
Garbage Pickup			-
Telephone HM & Cell	250		3,000
Cable/Sat.TV/Internet			-
Security Systems	30		360
Pool Service			-
Lawn, Pest & Repair Svc.	120		1,440
Maid Service			-
Maintenance			-
Property Taxes			-
Pest/Bug Service			-
Other			-
Total	1,750	-	21,000
Children Expenses			
Support Payments			-
Daycare	300		3,600
Activities		600	600
Other			-
Total	300	600	4,200
Transportation			
Loan/Lease	400		4,800
Gas	250		3,000
Maintenance		1,200	1,200
Tags/Inspection		120	120
Total	650	1,320	9,120
Food/Beverages			
Groceries	800		9,600
Household Supplies			-
Wine/Beer/etc.			-
Other			-
Total	800	-	9,600

	Monthly	Annual	Annualized Expense
Clothing			
Applicant		1,200	1,200
Co Applicant		600	600
Other		600	600
Total	-	2,400	2,400
Furnishings			
Inside		1,200	1,200
Outside			-
Total	-	1,200	1,200
Vacations and Holidays			
Travel Tickets		1,200	1,200
Hotels		600	600
Food		600	600
Entertainment		600	600
Auto		600	600
Other			-
Total	-	3,600	3,600
Gifts			
Holidays		800	800
Birthdays		300	300
Weddings		100	100
Other			-
Total	-	1,200	1,200
Personal Care and Cash			
Dry Cleaning	50		600
Hair/Nails/Facials	75		900
Cosmetics	25		300
Shoe Repair			-
Massage			
Health Club	35		420
Cash	400		4,800
Total	585	-	7,020
Medical/Dental/Prescriptions			
Vision		300	300
Co-pay		300	300
Deductible		400	400
Medication/Vitamins		400	400
Other			-
Total	-	1,400	1,400
Education/Self-Improvement			
Private School/College			-
Classes			-
Hobbies			-
Association Fees		200	200
Other			-
Total	-	200	200

Sample Budget

Client Name: John and Susan Johnson

	Monthly	Annual	Annualized Expense		Monthly	Annual	Annualized Expense
Installment Debt Payments				**General Insurance**			
Student Loans	100		1,200	Liability Insurance			
Visa	100		1,200	Policy 1			-
MasterCard	100		1,200	Policy 2			-
Other			-	**Total**	-	-	
Total	300	-	3,600	**Homeowners Insurance**			
Entertainment				Policy 1			-
Dining Out	200		2,400	Policy 2			-
Sports Tickets			-	**Total**	-	-	
Magazines			-	**Medical Insurance**			
Golf, etc.			-	Policy 1			-
Movies/Videos	50		600	Policy 2			-
Clubs Memberships			-	**Total**	-	-	
Other			-	**Auto Insurance**			
Total	250	-	3,000	Policy 1	200		2,400
Reinvested Dividends and Distribution				Policy 2			-
Total				**Total**	200	-	2,400
Pets				**Other Insurance**			
Food	50		600	Policy 1 (Vision)			-
Veterinarian		600	600	Policy 2 (Dental)			-
Other			-	Policy 3			-
Total	50	600	1,200	**Total**		-	
Miscellaneous				**TOTAL EXPENSES**	6,585	13,720	92,740
Family Support/Alimony		1,200	1,200				
Personal Computer			-		Monthly	Annual	
Other			-	**Income**			
Total	-	1,200	1,200	Net Salary (self)	4,600		55,200
Self Employment Taxes				Net Salary (spouse)	3,200		38,400
Taxes			-	Pension (self)			-
Other			-	Pension (spouse)			-
Total	-	-		Rental Income			-
Life Insurance				Investment Income			-
Policy 1	100		1,200	Child Support			-
Policy 2			-	Income Misc.			-
Total	100	-	1,200	**Total Income**	7,800	-	93,600
Disability Insurance							
Policy 1			-	**Disposable Income**			860
Policy 2			-				
Total	-	-					
Long Term Care							
Policy 1			-				
Policy 2			-				
Total	-	-					

Converting the Sample Budget to Create Your Ideal Budget

Use the sample budget and convert it to fit your lifestyle. Enter only the information that applies to you. The goal for this process is to use the information obtained from your ideal budget to create a master budget that matches the income and expenses as they occur in your life.

Now that you understand this process, it's time for you to create your master budget. The master budget is the combination of your monthly expenses and your quarterly or annual expenses. I will lead you through a step-by-step process of converting your expenses and income to your master budget.

Listing Expenses

The first step in the process is to separate the expenses you have identified in the sample budget into monthly expenses and annual expenses. See Step 1 of the budget sheet opposite.

Step 1 - Budget Sheet: Listing Expenses John & Susan Johnson		
	Monthly	Annual
Personal Savings	800	
Charitable Contributions	800	
Mortgage/Rent	1,000	
Community Dues	100	
Electricity	250	
Telephone/Cell/ Internet	250	
Security System	30	
Lawn Services	120	
Daycare	300	
Children's Activities		600
Car Payments	400	
Gas	250	
Car Maintenance		1200
AutoTag/Inspection		120
Groceries	800	
Clothing		2,400
Furnishings		1,200
Vacations/Holidays		3,600
Gifts		1,200
Personal Care	185	
Cash	400	
Vision		300
Co-pay		300
Deductible		400
Medication/Vitamins		400
Hobbies		200
Student Loans	100	
Visa	100	
MasterCard	100	
Dining Out	200	
Movies/Videos	50	
Pet Food	50	
Veterinarian		600
Family Support/Alimony		1,200
Life Insurance	100	
Auto Insurance	200	
Total Expenses	**$6,585**	**$13,720**

Next, add a column and label it "Due Date." Sort your expenses into monthly and annual expense groups. Get a copy of all your monthly bills and list the dates due on the budget sheet. Divide annual expenses by 12 to put them in monthly terms. This is what you will have to save each month so you can pay the annual expenses when they come due. Use the Step Two example as your model.

Step 2 - Budget Sheet: Add Due Date John & Susan Johnson			
Due Date		**Monthly**	**Annual**
15	Personal Savings	800	
1	Charitable Contributions	800	
28	Mortgage/Rent	1,000	
1	Community Dues	100	
15	Electricity	250	
12	Telephone/Cell/Internet	250	
28	Security System	30	
1	Lawn Services	120	
1	Daycare	300	
15	Car Payments	400	
1	Gas	250	
1	Groceries	800	
1	Personal Care	185	
1	Cash	400	
17	Student Loans	100	
5	Visa	100	
7	MasterCard	100	
1	Dining Out	200	
1	Movies/Videos	50	
1	Pet Food	50	
15	Life Insurance	100	
17	Auto Insurance	200	
	Total Monthly Expenses	**$6,585**	
	Children's Activities		600
	Car Maintenance		1,200
	AutoTag/Inspection		120
	Clothing		2,400
	Furnishings		1,200
	Vacations/Holidays		3,600
	Gifts		1,200
	Vision		300
	Co-pay		300
	Deductible		400
	Medication/Vitamins		400
	Hobbies		200
	Veterinarian		600
	Family Support/Alimony		1,200
	Total Annual Expenses		**$13,720**
15	Divide total quarterly or annual expenses by 12 to get monthly savings for quarterly or annual expenses.		**$1,143**

Matching Your Expenses and Income

Decide whether to use the 1st or the 15th of the month for quarterly or annual expenses based on your income and the amount of monthly expenses. Now that we know what your monthly savings for annual expenses must be, we can complete your master budget.

The next step is to add a column for income. Most people get paid at least twice per month. We want to separate your expenses that are paid monthly to match your monthly income. Study the following Master Budget sample.

Sample Master Budget: Matching Your Expenses and Income John & Susan Johnson				
Due Date		Monthly Expenses		Monthly Income
1	Charitable Contributions	800		2,300
1	Community Dues	100		1,600
1	Lawn Services	120		
1	Daycare	300		
1	Gas	250		
1	Groceries	800		
1	Personal Care	185		
1	Cash	400		
1	Dining Out	200		
1	Movies/Videos	50		
1	Pet Food	50		
5	Visa	100		
7	MasterCard	100		
12	Telephone/Cell/Internet	250		
	Subtotal	$3,705		$3,900
15	Personal Savings	800		2,300
15	Electricity	250		1,600
15	Car Payments	400		
15	Life Insurance	100		
15	Savings for Quarterly or Annual Expeses	1,143		
17	Student Loans	100		
17	Auto Insurance	200		
28	Mortgage/Rent	1,000		
28	Security System	30		
	Subtotal	$4,023		$3,900
	Grand Total	$7,728		$7,800

Expenses that are weekly needs, like gas for the car, groceries, dining out, and cash for small purchases, should be listed on the first of the month. In the next column of this sheet, you should list the date you receive net (after tax) income. The ideal model is the income that you receive on the 1st through the 15th of the month should be paying expenses for the 16th through the 30th of the month. This gives you a two-week cushion to always pay your bills on time. This process has been great for a number of clients because it relieves the stress of having to pay late fees when bills are paid past their due dates.

Problems with Executing a Budget

There are a number of problems associated with executing a budget, and the whole process at times seems overwhelming. There is nothing too difficult for you to overcome if you just keep it simple. I've seen budgets so detailed that you get lost in the information. On the other hand, I have seen budgets where not enough information is captured, so too much of the information is unknown. The ideal budget is one in which you capture enough information, with as little effort as possible, to get a realistic picture of how you spend money. I encourage my clients to use cash as little as possible. It is easier to capture monthly expenses with either a credit card, a debit card, or by writing a check.

When clients spend cash, sometimes the information about how the funds are spent is not always recorded. The easiest way to keep track of cash is to withdraw the same amount of cash on a weekly basis. It doesn't matter how the money is spent and you don't have to track it. If you withdraw $200 per week, and at the end of the week, you have no money left, you know that you just spent $200. When you withdraw funds from the ATM multiple times during the week, it is difficult to keep track of how much cash is spent. The problem is that clients, on occasion, forget to list their ATM transactions in their checkbook register. This could lead to your account being overdrawn, which produces additional banking fees. Start out by getting the same amount every week. If it's not enough, then get more the next week, and if it's too much, then get a little less. Over time, you will find the right amount of cash needed for your family each week.

You can create a problem by using your debit card or credit card to buy items that only cost a few dollars because it's hard to keep up with these transactions. As a general rule, don't use your debit card or credit card for purchases under $10. I've had clients who forgot to list small transactions, such as buying lunch on their debit card, only to find out later that they have overdrawn their checking accounts. By the time they get notification from their bank, they have already exceeded their balances by several transactions. In some cases, each of the overdrawn transactions resulted in fees of $25 to $35. Paying $40 to $70 dollars in bank fees to buy a hamburger, just because you failed to list the debit transaction in your checkbook register, is a costly lesson. If you decide to purchase items with your debit card, you must make it a habit to list these transactions in your checkbook register. Take this as an opportunity to learn from other people's mistakes and not create the same error yourself.

Your Family Bank

Have you noticed that the neighborhood bank has been around for a long time? Why not use it as an example for creating your own family bank. A part of the budget is designed for long-term savings, such as college funding, retirement, or the down payment for a new car or home.

Another part of the budget is designed for short-term needs. These items are expenses that will occur within a one-year period, but may not occur every month. Examples are the escrow for property taxes and homeowner's insurance, (if it is not included in your mortgage), funds for summer activities for the kids, back to school clothing and supplies, maintenance repairs for your automobile, vacations, and gifts.

If you pay your property taxes yearly, it's amazing how the taxing authority always remembers to send you a bill once a year. If you shop for gifts at Christmas, wow, it's amazing that Christmas always comes every December! These events can be treated as random events, or you can plan for them. For example, let's look at property taxes. If your annual property tax is $3,600, you should divide that amount by 12. That means that $300 a month should be set aside in the savings account until the funds are needed.

Look over the sample expenses that might not occur every month, but usually occur within a year.

Expense	Annual Amount	Monthly Amount
Children's Activities	600	50
Car Expenses	1,320	110
Clothing	2,400	200
Furnishings	1,200	100
Vacation	3,600	300
Gifts	1,200	100
Medical Expenses	1,400	117
Hobbies	200	17
Pet Expenses	600	50
Family Support/Alimony	1,200	100
Total	**$13,720**	**$1,144**

Based on the budget above, $1,144 should be withdrawn from your take-home pay and set aside each month, to cover expenses anticipated during the year. If possible, have the monies for your *Family Bank* automatically withdrawn from your paycheck and deposited into an account separate from your regular checking or saving accounts. If you combine the money with your regular saving and checking funds, you could easily make the mistake of thinking that you have extra money. The reality is, you don't. These funds are set aside for those future expenses that you know are coming, expenses that might be difficult to pay if you had not prepared for them. The only expenses paid from this savings account would be the quarterly and annual expenses.

Okay, I know that I just said that this contingency fund is set aside exclusively for anticipated expenditures, but in an emergency, you can borrow from these banked funds. For example, let's look at your vacation fund. If you set aside $3,600 for your vacation that was planned for December, but you have a car repair expense of $3,000 in April, you can borrow the money from your vacation funds and pay yourself back by December. By creating your own bank, you are able to borrow from yourself at a fraction of the cost of putting the additional expense on a credit card. By establishing the family bank, individuals can survive financial hardships. This process encourages you to stay within your plan and avoid placing extra expenses on credit cards.

If you are not saving as you should, how do you begin? Create your family bank by committing to save 50 percent of all future salary increases until you reach your desired saving goal. If you are saving two percent of your income, and you expect to earn a raise of at least four percent, over a five-year period, you will gradually grow from saving two percent of your income to ten percent of your income.

Think about starting to exercise. If you haven't been exercising for a while, it's hard to run five miles overnight. However, if you gradually increase your exercise from walking to running, you'll eventually get comfortable with running a greater distance. As your income grows over the years, you should be able to save 20 percent or more of your income.

This is a perfect time to move to the next section, "Using Credit Cards or Debit Cards".

Summary

- List expenses and income by date to identify cash flow differences.
- Funds should go to a saving account directly from your paycheck.
- Create your own family bank.

CHAPTER 5

Using Credit Cards or Debit Cards

ADVANTAGES

USING a credit card or debit card has advantages. It's convenient and it's easier to use than writing a check. Some merchants, who won't accept checks, because they don't want to take a chance that they'll be returned, will only accept credit cards or debit cards. For purchases over $300, I usually recommend to clients that they use a credit card instead of writing a check or paying cash. This works as a safeguard. For purchases covered under a manufacturer's warranty, you are required to show proof of purchase during the warranty period. If you lose your receipt, you can always retrieve a copy of the receipt from your credit card company. Another important reason to use a credit card for purchases is to validate proof of purchases after a major loss, such as a fire, flood, tornado, or hurricane.

Early in my banking career, one of the areas in which I worked was disaster recovery. I learned that the bank had back-up computers that maintained duplicate records of all transactions at a secured facility. In a catastrophe, we could reproduce records of all our transactions. We also kept electronic records and photocopies of furniture and office equipment inventory. This gave me the idea of creating an inventory of the items in my home.

I kept an electronic spreadsheet of all purchases of $300 or more, along with the original receipt attached to the credit card statement. I later started keeping a photocopy of these items as part of my inventory. After hurricane Andrew in August of 1992, with these records I was able to quickly settle my claim with my insurance company because I had proof of purchase to support most items listed on my claim. Our home was among one of the first to be repaired after the hurricane. That Thanksgiving dinner remains one of the most meaningful dinners we shared in our home because it was one of the first meals we had there after it was rebuilt following the devastation of hurricane Andrew.

Another reason to use a credit card or debit card for purchases is that it's safer than carrying large amounts of cash. It's not only safer for you but also for the merchants. Merchants fear the risk of accepting counterfeit bills and dislike the added cost of security to have armored cars pick up large amounts of cash at the end of the business day. They also fear the risk to either themselves or their employees of being robbed while taking cash deposits to the local bank.

Disadvantages

Using a credit card or debit card also has disadvantages. A credit card in the hands of the unwary user is a big problem. A credit card makes it easy to make purchases. The problem with a credit card is that if you spend more than you can afford to pay off when the statement comes, the interest makes it very costly.

The major disadvantage of using a debit card is that if you fail to keep track of these transactions they could lead to additional banking fees if you overdraw your checking account.

Look at the chart below. The average credit card interest rate is around 20 percent. If you are in the 25 percent income tax bracket, for each dollar you earn, only 75 cents is taken home in your paycheck because income taxes are taken out first. Therefore, you are using 75 cents for each dollar earned to pay back debt on your credit card. This means that you have to earn $1.60 to pay back every $1.00 you spend on a credit card. If you are carrying a balance on your credit card, normally you should stop making additional purchases on it.

Cost of Using Credit Cards Chart

Credit Card Purchase	Credit Card Interest Rate	Total Cost = Purchase Cost + Interest
$1.00	20%	$1.20
Income	Sample Income Tax Bracket	After Tax Income
$1.00	25%	$0.75

$$\frac{\text{Total Cost}}{\text{After Tax Income}} = \frac{\$1.20}{\$0.75} = \$1.60 \text{ (Total cost including interest)}$$

To calculate your cost of credit card usage, substitute your credit card interest rate and your income tax bracket.

Another disadvantage of using credit cards occurs when you make late payments. A late payment, or having too much debt in relation to your income, decreases your credit score, damaging your credit rating. A poor credit rating sometimes makes it harder to get lower interest rates in the future. Some employers use your credit history as part of their background check, which could prevent you from getting a job in some industries. Managing your debts and paying your bills on time is a vital part of using credit.

Summary

- **Advantages of using a credit card or debit card**
  Convenient
  Accepted by merchants in most places
  Good for verification of purchases
  Safer than carrying cash

- **Disadvantages of using a credit card**
  Interest charges make it costly
  Late payments increase cost
  Bad idea to carry a balance

- **Disadvantage of using a debit card**
  Additional banking fees if not used properly

Establishing a Debt Reduction Plan

If you have multiple credit cards with balances, there is an effective way to pay off those credit cards. The following is a technique that I have shared with a number of clients that helped them to pay off their credit card debt.

First, gather your credit card statements and make a list of the following information: name of credit card, minimum payment, current balance, available balance, and interest rate.

Step 1: List All Credit Card Information				
Name of Credit Card	**Minimum Payment**	**Current Balance**	**Available Balance**	**Interest Rate**
MasterCard	$200	$14,000	$6,000	16.99%
VISA	$100	$5,000	$5,000	19.99%
Macy's	$50	$800	$1,200	18.00%
Sears	$50	$200	$1,800	18.00%
VISA	$150	$12,500	$7,500	9.99%
Target	$50	$315	$1,685	18.00%

List the information in order of the cards with the smallest balance first.

Step 2: Sort By Balance, List Smallest Balance First				
Name of Credit Card	**Minimum Payment**	**Current Balance**	**Available Balance**	**Interest Rate**
Sears	$50	$200	$1,800	18.00%
Target	$50	$315	$1,685	18.00%
Macy's	$50	$800	$1,200	18.00%
VISA	$100	$5,000	$5,000	19.99%
VISA	$150	$12,500	$7,500	9.99%
MasterCard	$200	$14,000	$6,000	16.99%

Transfer balances, where possible, to the cards that have available credit with the lower interest rates. Those credit cards with the higher interest rates should be destroyed and those accounts closed.

Step 3: Consolidate Accounts with Higher Interest Rate to Credit Cards with Lower Interest Rate				
Name of Credit Card	Minimum Payment	Current Balance	Available Balance	Interest Rate
Sears	$50	$200	$1,800	18.00%
Target	$50	$315	$1,685	18.00%
MasterCard	$200	$14,000	$6,000	16.99%
VISA	$200	$18,300	$1,700	9.99%

A common mistake people make when paying off credit card debt is paying extra money on the credit card with the largest balance. This may reduce that account balance, but it may not reduce your minimum monthly payments for that credit card. The best thing to do is make the extra payment against the credit card with the lowest balance. When you pay it off, you will increase your cash flow because you are no longer receiving the bill for that credit card.

Step 4: Establish Payment Reduction Schedule							
Name of Credit Card	Minimum Payment	Extra Payment Plus Previous Minimim Payment	Maximum Funds Available for New Monthly Payment	Paid of in Months	Current Balance	Available Credit	Interest Rate
Extra Funds		$200					
Sears	$50	$200	$250	1	$200	$1,800	18.00%
Target	$50	$250	$300	2	$315	$1,685	18.00%
MasterCard	$200	$300	$500	33	$14,000	$6,000	16.99%
Visa	$200	$500	$700	53	$18,300	$1,200	9.99%
Total	$600		$700		$32,815		

In the example above, all the credit card debts can be paid off in around five years. The extra payment of $200 per month is applied to the credit card with the lowest current balance. The extra funds of $200 are added to the current minimum payment of $50 to increase the maximum funds available to pay off debts. The Sears balance is $200; therefore, it will be paid off in one month. Once the Sears balance is paid off, apply the $250 that was available to Sears to the Target balance. Now Target will be paid off in the second month.

Pretend you are still paying the Sears and Target bills and apply the maximum funds available to the MasterCard that now has the lowest balance. Three good things just happened. One, you are no longer getting bills from Sears and Target. Two, you have learned a way to pay off all your debts. Three, at the end of five years, you will have approximately $700 per month that could be added to your savings or used towards any new bill, without adding to any current credit card balances.

After paying off each debt, give yourself a little reward. This will encourage you to stick with your plan.

WAYS TO PAY OFF CREDIT CARD DEBT

A source of funds that might be less costly than using credit cards is your local credit union. Members of credit unions are able to get loans, including signature loans, at rates that may be lower than those of credit card companies. Credit unions are sometimes able to offer car loans at much lower interest rates than banks or some auto dealers because of their lower overhead costs.

Another source of funds might be a home equity line of credit. Homeowners who have equity in their homes may consider obtaining an equity line of credit against their home to pay off existing credit card debt. Normally the interest rate charged on a home equity loan is lower than the rate charged for credit cards. In addition, the interest that is charged against your equity line is usually tax deductible; be sure to consult a tax specialist to see if this can work for you. The minimum payment required on an equity line is usually lower than the payments on credit card. When you acquire an equity loan, you should make the same higher payments that you were paying for the credit cards. This way you can pay off the equity line even faster.

It has taken a long time to create this financial problem, so you are not going to pay off all the debts overnight. This is a slow process, but it works. As you pay down your debt, it's a good time for self-analysis, to determine how you got into this problem in the first place. The discipline that it takes to get out of this problem is the same discipline that will help you save for your retirement or for college funding for your children.

For some people, debt problems were caused by unnecessary spending, such as taking a vacation they could not afford or buying clothing to keep pace with current trends. For others, the absence of an emergency fund meant that using credit cards was the only way to cover unexpected costs. Regardless of the reason, being aware of the problem is the first step towards the solution. Make a pledge to resist these temptations and follow your new budget so you don't fall back into those old spending habits.

Now that you have found a way to pay off your credit card balances, this doesn't give you the green light to charge unnecessary purchases. By following a disciplined approach to paying off debts, in five years you should have enough money to invest on a monthly basis.

MANAGING YOUR CREDIT CARD NEEDS

Many people don't realize that the mistakes made with credit cards have a long-lasting impact. For example, many companies use credit checks as a part of their job screening process prior to employment. If you have extensive credit card debt or a history of paying late, employers might think that this could impact your decision-making ability. For instance, it would be difficult to get a job in the financial service industry if you have a bad credit history. Your employer might have a concern that your need for income could lead you to make decisions that is in your best interest instead of your client's.

A common mistake that many people make with credit cards is that they believe they need to have a large number of them. In most cases, you don't need more than three credit cards. For example, you may need one Visa card, one MasterCard and one American Express card. Most businesses will accept one of these credit cards, eliminating the need to have a credit card for each major store. Many stores offer promotions giving you an additional discount if you purchase with the store credit card. In the long run, this just encourages you to make unnecessary purchases.

A number of my clients use the "three credit cards" concept. One card is used for personal items, the second is used for business purchases, and the third is used for business mileage. This practice separates your personal items from your business items and provides a clear accounting system for your income tax records. For this practice to work, you must always separate business and personal items and use the right card.

Summary

- Credit card usage for major purchases makes it easier to retrieve lost receipts for insurance purposes.
- Interest charges for not paying the entire balance in full and late payment fees can be very costly.
- Establish a debt reduction plan to pay off credit card debts.

- Consider credit union signature loans or home equity loans as an alternative to credit cards.
- Reduce the number of credit cards that you use.

Our next chapter reviews factors to take in consideration when making the decision to buy cars.

CHAPTER 6

Buying Cars

L ET'S turn to another area—buying cars. One might ask what buying cars have to do with creating wealth. Creating wealth is a way of accumulating assets that appreciate in value. Cars are not appreciating assets; they depreciate or lose value over time. It's nice to have the car of your dreams, but it doesn't necessarily have to be the first one you buy. The less money you spend on depreciating assets, the more wealth you will create.

Emotional Influences

For most people, the decision of which car to buy is an emotional one, based on how the car looks, because it has a certain style, or because of certain colors. Some people are influenced by their high school or college colors. Others may be influenced by the colors of their organizations. How the car drives is often a decision factor, and car dealers use this to their advantage. This is why they always want you to take a test drive. Once you start driving the car and you fall in love with it, you start to convince yourself that this is the right one. Once the dealer realizes that you are in love with the car, the dealer might use this emotion to get you to buy the car.

Factors to Consider Before Buying a Car

On the other hand, wealthy people take a different approach when deciding on how or when a car should be purchased. In most cases, they don't make decisions on impulse; they do their homework and take several factors into consideration when buying cars.

From a functionality point of view, wealthy clients consider how many passengers will be using the car. For example, are they just a family of two? Will this be the only family car, or will they have two cars? What about one luxury car and one practical car? Instead of buying two luxury cars, it may be best to buy one luxury car and one practical car, and use the additional funds for other needs.

The other functionality factor is how you will use the vehicle. Some people may consider a sports utility vehicle (SUV) because they take many trips and may need additional space for stowing luggage. Others may use it to pull a boat and need more power compared to a car. Some people may use their cars for business purposes and are able to deduct some of the costs of operating the vehicle. This leads us to another factor in the buying decision: the cost of operating the vehicle.

There are three main costs of operating a car: gasoline, maintenance, and insurance. Due to the increasing cost of gasoline, the average miles per gallon of gas have become a significant factor when deciding which car to buy. If you plan to drive many miles, you definitely want to consider a car that is gasoline-efficient. Maintenance includes such costs as tire replacement and major and minor repairs. Can you do these repairs, or must they be done by an authorized dealer/mechanic? The cost to maintain a luxury car is significantly greater than an economical car. Finally, the hidden factor in buying a car that is often overlooked is the cost of car insurance. Two similar cars that are rated differently can have quite different insurance costs. Just before making the final decision, call an automobile insurance company and get a quote.

Another factor in the car-buying decision is whether to buy or lease it. The answer to this question is simple for most people. Leased cars usually have a stated number of miles in the contract (between 12,000 to 15,000 miles per year). If you normally drive more miles than the lease provides, then it may not be to your advantage to lease the car, since most dealers charge you for each mile you drive over your leased agreement. This is similar to a telephone package, where you get a certain number of minutes per month. The cost gets very high for each minute you use your telephone over your allotted minutes per month. However, if you like to change cars every two to three years and not worry about the maintenance cost as the car gets older, then you may want to consider a lease.

If you decide to buy a car, do you buy a new or used one? Most cars depreciate in value the most during its first year. For this reason, you may want to buy a new car just before the next year's model is released. One of the best times to buy a car is at the end of the year. Most dealers get incentives from the manufacturers to sell a certain number of cars each year, and they might be willing to lower the cost of the cars to sell more, so they can meet their annual goals. Many dealers also have incentives to sell the older model inventory to make room for the newer cars. The dealers sometime give offers such as no maintenance cost for the first four years, which is a big savings to you and at a low cost for them.

Some people like to lease a new car every year and return the old one to the dealer. These cars sometimes create an opportunity to get a great deal on a used car. The car dealers thoroughly inspect the cars and sell them with warranties comparable to those for a new car. This creates a win-win situation for you and the dealer. The car dealer gets to sell more cars, and you, as the buyer, get the peace of mind that comes from buying a used car with a "new car" warranty. The main factor behind all these buying decisions is that the less money you spend, the closer you will get to accumulating wealth.

Summary

- Avoid buying cars based on emotional decisions.
- Factors to consider before buying a car include: functionality, cost of operating the car, and cost of buying the car.
- If possible, time the purchase of your car to meet the year-end sales.

As I travel around the country and give seminars, another topic that generates a lot of interest is investing. Let's take a closer look at that in the next chapter.

CHAPTER 7

Investing

INVESTING is a topic that many people don't understand. My goal is to increase your understanding in this area so that you can feel comfortable with investing in stocks, bonds and mutual funds. Let's use an analogy that most people can relate to. Pretend that you don't know how to swim. I'm going to place you in a swimming pool where the water is no deeper than three to five feet. Since you are probably taller than five feet, it is unlikely that you will drown in such shallow water. If you become uncomfortable, you can just stand up. Once you realize your fear is unnecessary, you start to relax.

I can remember when my son was two years old, and my wife and I wanted him to learn how to swim. We hired a lifeguard to give him private lessons, and I can still remember hearing him scream that he didn't want to get into the pool. After playing in the water for a few minutes with the lifeguard, he started to have fun. It was amazing to me that after a few lessons, he was diving into the deep end of the pool instead of screaming and being afraid of getting into the water. I have observed this transformation with clients. I have seen clients fight and resist learning about investing in stocks, bonds, and mutual funds. As they began to learn how to invest and became comfortable putting their money into the stock market, they overcame their fears.

Financial professionals help you learn to swim comfortably in the investment arena.

Basic Lessons About Investing

- In order to invest you must have money. If you spend all the money you earn, then even if you discover a good investment opportunity, you couldn't invest because your investment funds are gone.
- A good rule of investing is to pay yourself first and create some savings.
- Create an emergency fund that is about three to six times your monthly expenses, to cover expenses for your family bank.
- Calculate your expected rate of return before you start to invest.
- If the interest rate of your current debts is greater than your expected return on your investment, then you should pay your current debts off before investing.
- Seek the opinions of others who are knowledgeable in the area in which you are considering. You can get the thoughts of others while getting your hair cut at the barbershop. Remember, everyone has an opinion, but everyone isn't an expert on what they talk about.

Ground Rules About Investing

Financial literacy is seldom taught in schools. Students are taught how to run companies, but little time is spent on teaching individuals how to manage their personal finances. I have a high school degree, a bachelor's degree and a master's degree, but there were no courses in personal financial skills. Not until I participated in an investment club and started studying for my securities licenses did I become aware of how to invest.

Let's clear up a misunderstanding about investing. My

experience would lead me to estimate that perhaps 80 percent of the population needs help with their financial affairs. If you went to a football stadium and placed all the people who understand how to invest on one end of the field, you might only fill the space between the end zone and the 20-yard line. If you are fortunate to be in the group that understands investments, you can be a great resource in assisting other family members and friends to become a part of your group. All the remaining people in the stadium need help with their financial affairs. The truth is, you are not alone in how you feel about investing. However, if you no longer wish to be like many others, I am willing to share as much information as possible to get you into the group that understands investments.

I would encourage you not to do this on your own. If you are a spiritual person, I would encourage you to pray for guidance. I would also encourage you to form a support group, where you can encourage each other as you grow financially. Without encouragement, it's easy to fall back to your old ways and not expend the extra effort that's necessary to change. I can remember when I was trying to lose weight. When I first started going to the gym, it was a struggle to get there. Some days I didn't feel like exercising, but with the aid of a personal trainer I stayed motivated. I learned how to use the machines and develop habits that are now part of my daily life. Gaining financial literacy is also a life-changing experience. Once you know how to invest, your life will be different forever.

One of the keys to successful investing is to separate your investments into short-term and long-term time horizons:

Short-term time horizon: Generally for periods up to two years
Current living expenses
Savings for quarterly and annual expenses
Current income

Long-term time horizon: Generally for periods greater than two years

  Growth
  Aggressive Growth
  Future Income

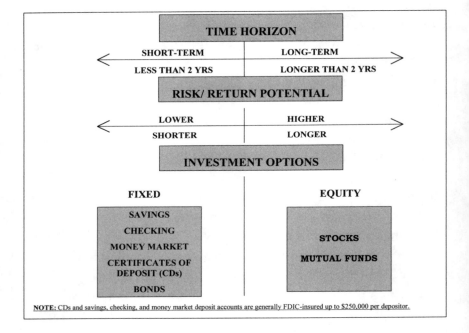

NOTE: CDs and savings, checking, and money market deposit accounts are generally FDIC-insured up to $250,000 per depositor.

MATCH INVESTMENTS TO YOUR TIME HORIZONS

As a financial professional, I normally suggest that my clients place their funds in three "buckets" of money. The first bucket covers expenses that will occur within a twelve-month period. You cannot afford to risk the principal of these funds. These funds normally cover current living expenses, savings for annual expenses, and current income. These funds should be placed in fixed accounts such as savings, checking, money market accounts, and certificates of deposit.

The second bucket of funds covers expenses that will occur in a 12 to 24 months period. For example, you may be saving funds for the down payment towards the purchase of a home. You've estimated that this will take you two years. It is more important to consider when you'll need these funds, rather than the potential returns you could achieve. A fixed instrument pays a certain rate of return for a stated time period, and you can estimate with a high degree of accuracy what the expected rate of return should be.

Your third bucket of funds is designed for time horizons generally greater than two years. These funds need to grow for future income, to pay for retirement or college, for example. A portion of these funds can be invested in equities, such as stocks and equity mutual funds. These funds are designed to offer you the potential to keep up with taxes and inflation, which will likely increase over time. Therefore, to help ensure that your investments don't lose buying power in the future, it needs to grow at a rate greater than inflation.

Fixed investments and equities have different historical rates of return. One guide used by investment professionals is the following Ibbotson chart, which provides a historical insight into the performance of various asset classes over time.

Ibbotson SBBI Stocks, Bonds, Bills and Inflation 1926-2008	
Compound Annual Return	
• Small Stocks	11.7%**
• Large Stocks	9.6%**
• Long-Term Govt Bonds	5.7%*
• Treasury Bills	3.7%*
• Inflation	3.0%*

* Government bonds and Treasury bills are guaranteed by the full faith and credit of the United States government as to the timely payment of principal and interest, while stocks are not guaranteed and have been more volatile that the other asset classes. Furthermore, small stocks are more volatile than large stocks, and subject to significant price fluctuations and business risks, and are thinly traded.

** Source: Small stocks-represented by the fifth capitalization quintile of stocks on the NYSE for 1926-1981 and the performance of the Dimensional Fund Advisors (DFA) U.S. Micro Cap Portfolio thereafter, Large Stocks—standard & Poor's 500®, which is an unmanaged group of securities and considered to be representative of the stock market in general; Long-Term Government Bonds—20 year U.S. government Bond; treasury Bills—30-day U.S. treasury Bill; Inflation—Consumer Price Index.

This is for illustrative purposes only and not indicative of the performance of any specific investment product or portfolio. The data assumes reinvestment of all income and does not account for taxes or transaction costs. The average return represents a compound annual return. Bonds in a portfolio are typically intended to provide income and/or investment in asset classes different from stocks. U.S. Government bonds may be exempt from state taxes, and income is taxed as ordinary income in the year received. With government bonds, the investor is a creditor of the government. Government bonds and Treasury bills are guaranteed by the full faith and credit of the United States government as to the timely payment of principal and interest. For government securities, government guarantees apply to the underlying securities of the portfolio and not to the value of the portfolio shares.

Bond investments are subject to interest rate risk so that when interest rates rise, the prices of bonds can decrease and the investor can lose principal value. Stocks are not guaranteed and have been more volatile than the other asset classes. Large company stocks provide ownership in corporations that intend to provide growth and or current income. Even though large cap stocks are perceived to be less risky than smaller cap companies, they still involve risks, i.e., they will fluctuate in value and you can lose money. Small company stocks provide ownership in corporations that intend to seek high levels of growth. Furthermore, small stocks are more volatile and have less liquidity than large stocks, are subject to significant price fluctuations and business risks, and are thinly traded. Capital gains and dividends may be taxed in the year received. An investment cannot be made directly in an index. Past performance is not guarantee of future results.

Pretend that you're a disc jockey, and you're hired to play music at a large company holiday party. Your job is to entertain the people and make sure everyone has a good time. If you do a good job, they'll hire you to play for them in the future. The pressure is on; you want to make sure everyone has the time of their lives. Have you ever gone to a party where the DJ is playing music but nobody is dancing? Boring! The people are thinking, "What am I doing here? I can't wait for this party to be over."

Most people don't realize that playing music is an art. The key to having a successful party is to find out what music people like. Everyone listens to radio station "WII FM": "What's in it for me?" The job of the DJ is to let the guests tune into their "radio station." The best way to do this is to take requests. For some people it's old school music. They may want to hear Michael Jackson's "Shake Your Body Down to the Ground" or "Thriller." For others it might be country music: Alabama's "Play Me Some Mountain Music," while your Caribbean brothers and sisters may want to hear Arrow's, "Hot, Hot, Hot." For people who like Latin music, they may enjoy listening to Gloria Estefan & Miami Sound Machine "Conga". Others who may be more spiritual may want to hear Marvin Sapp's, "Never Could Have Made It." The only way for a DJ to know the audience's favorite songs is to ask.

Just as a DJ plays a variety of music to please your guests, investment professionals use a variety of asset classes to help you design a portfolio that's suitable and appropriate for you. A well-designed portfolio often includes fixed investments for short-term time horizons as well as equities for long-term time horizons. All investments compete against taxes and inflation. It is important to have the right balance between fixed and equity investments. History has taught us that a large portion of an individual invest-ment portfolio performance is often determined by its level of diversification by asset class. The key point to understand is that it takes a variety of music to please your party guests, and it takes a variety of asset classes of funds to help you make your portfolio successful over time.

(See chart on page 79)

Investments on the fixed side range from savings accounts to investment grade bonds. While these investments can provide a relative degree of safety, their performance over the long term may not fully meet your needs after taxes and inflation are taken into account. For example, if you are in a 25 percent tax bracket and invested in a hypothetical certificate of deposit (CD) that is paying 4 percent, 1 percent is set aside for taxes. If we assume inflation is at 3.5 percent, your CD must pay at least 4.5 percent to keep pace with taxes and inflation. While it appears safe that your principal is not going down, you are actually losing buying power. The income earned from your CD may not be keeping pace with the increased costs of living due to inflation and taxes. It's important to remember that, unlike equity or debt investments, CDs are generally FDIC-insured up to $250,000 per depositor. Depending on your situation, the funds that should be invested in short-term fixed instruments are those that are necessary to cover both monthly and annual expenses.

TAXES:	1.0%
INFLATION:	3.5%
TOTAL	**4.5%**

UNDERSTANDING STOCKS AND BONDS

For periods of time longer than two years, equity investments can help the investor keep pace with taxes and inflation over the long term. A well-designed portfolio can include equity investments (stocks or mutual funds) to address a variety of investment styles and objectives such as:

Small, medium, and large size companies
Domestic and international companies
Growth and value style companies
Specialty sectors, such as health care, technology, and real estate

Having a diversified equity portfolio (funds invested in a variety of equity investments that tend to react differently to market movement) is very important because performance of different market sectors can vary during good and bad economic times. For example, it is possible that while small to medium sized companies are performing poorly, large sized companies could be performing well. Because of this, a diversified equity portfolio can help reduce the big fluctuations many people experience in the performance of their portfolios. As an example, if all your funds are invested in large companies, and they are doing well, this is great. However, if large companies are performing poorly, your entire portfolio will reflect that poor performance. If your portfolio contained smaller cap companies to balance it out, and the smaller companies happen to be performing better at the moment, your overall portfolio may not be as dramatically affected by the losses of its larger company stocks.

SHORT-TERM GENERALLY LESS THAN 2 YEARS

FIXED INVESTMENTS
Cash or Cash Equivalency / Bonds

Treasury Bills 3.7%*   Government Bonds 5.7%*

ME	SAE	CI

Cash or Cash Equivalent

Savings
Checking
Money Market
CDs

Treasury Bills 3.7%*
Government Bonds 5.7%*

* These figures are taken directly from the Ibbotson SBBI chart on page 74 and presented here as hypothetical and for illustrative purposes only. They are not intended to represent the performance of any specific investment. This example does not take into account the impact of any fees or taxes. Past performance is no guarantee of future results.

ME – Monthly Expenses	SAE – Savings for Annual Expenses	CI - Current Income

LONG-TERM GENERALLY GREATER THAN 2 YEARS

EQUITY INVESTMENTS
Stocks, Mutual Funds

Large Cap Stocks 9.6%*   Small Cap Stocks 11.7%*

ASSET CLASS

LCS	SCS

LCS

GROWTH STYLE	BLEND/ COMBINATION STYLE	VALUE STYLE
Large Cap	Large Cap Index	Large Cap

SCS

Mid Cap	Mid Cap Index	Mid Cap
Small Cap	Small Cap Index	Small Cap
International	International Index	International

Specialty
- Health
- Technology
- Real Estate

LCS – Large Cap Stocks   SCS– Small Cap Stocks

Differing stock types add balance to your portfolio and can help you withstand large fluctuations over the long term. For example, when international stocks are doing well, the United States (US) stocks (domestic stocks) may not be doing as well. An example of an international stock is Toyota, whose headquarters is located outside of the US, and an example of a domestic stock is Ford, a company whose headquarters is located in the US.

It's important to keep in mind that international securities carry additional risks, including currency exchange fluctuation and different government regulations, economic conditions, or accounting standards. Foreign securities may fall due to adverse political, social, and economic developments abroad; the risks of investing in emerging-market countries are greater than the risks generally associated with foreign investments. Stocks of growth companies differ from those of value companies in which returns come to the investor in the form of dividends, while growth companies tend to reward investors with the potential for the appreciation in the value of the company. Hypothetically speaking, while a large cap value stock of one company may not be performing well at a given time, the large cap stock of a growth company may be performing better. In this sense, these two investments in an investor's portfolio may serve to complement one another.

HOW INVESTING CAN WORK FOR YOU

Pretend you are going to a family reunion and you're driving from Miami to Atlanta. The minimum speed limit on the highway is 40 miles per hour (MPH) and the maximum speed limit is 60 MPH. If you were to compare driving to investing, your investment "speed" for short term is similar to a Treasury bill's 3.7 percent while your investment "speed" for long-term is 9.6 percent similar to large cap stocks. Given the speed limits, if you were to exceed the speed limit by say 50 percent, would you consider this speeding? (Hey, you are driving at 90 MPH in a 60 MPH zone!). This is also true with investing. If based on historical rates of return the investor can hope for certain percentage for a given investment over the long-term, but his or her portfolio is performing at a 50 percent higher rate at some point, we could consider this "speeding." These 3.7% and 9.6% figures are taken directly from the Ibbotson SBBI chart on page 74 and presented here as hypothetical for the purpose of illustrating my point. They do not represent the performance of any specific investment, nor do they take into account the impact of fees or taxes. Past performance is no guarantee of future results.

One of the keys to successful long-term investing is to determine for yourself, based on your financial situation, your tolerance for risk, and your time horizon, when the time is right to buy or sell a stock or mutual fund. If you were traveling in a foreign country and you did not completely understand the language well, you would still need to understand the time of day. This is the same with investing. You may not understand everything you need to know about investing, but you must still understand when buying or selling an investment may be best for you, given your current individual circumstances.

A watch has both a small and a big hand. Equate the small hand to when you might consider selling a stock or mutual fund when it is doing poorly. For example, if I am investing in Treasury bills without a lot of risk, I should hope for an even better rate over the same time period from the equity investment to compensate me for assuming the greater associated risk to my principal. If the return on the equity investment then exceeds my established rate of return by 50 percent, I may be "speeding" and might consider selling the shares at that point. The problem some people have is that they get emotionally attached to a stock or company and don't buy or sell the stock in a timely manner.

Rebalancing

Rebalancing is a tool that financial professionals use to help their clients adjust accounts. If your portfolio was designed to have 40 percent of your funds invested in fixed instruments and 60 percent of your funds in equity investments, your account will automatically adjust back to this allocation any time your investment performance has changed the proportion of your portfolio. This is like setting the cruise control in your car at 60 MPH. Anytime you drive up a hill it automatically speeds up your car, but when you are coming down a hill it slows your car down until you are back to 60 MPH. Automatic rebalancing attempts to do the same for your portfolio. In this example, when the equity portion of your portfolio exceeds 60 percent, the rebalancing process would automatically sell the amount greater than 60 percent and invest the difference in a fixed investment to get that back to the set amount of 40 percent. Rebalancing can be set to be done daily, monthly, quarterly, or as available within your portfolio.

The advantage of automatic rebalancing is that it takes emotion out of the decision-making process. The hardest time to convince someone to sell a stock or mutual fund is when it is performing well. In 2008, I knew a number of clients who were considering retiring and relocating to a smaller house during retirement. The clients met with their real estate agents and were advised to sell their homes, because the price was high at the time. However, some of the clients wanted to wait, because they thought the prices would continue to rise. In September of 2008, the stock market started to fall and real estate prices declined faster than anyone anticipated. Those clients who waited lost out. It may be best to set your expected rate of returns and buy or sell the investment when you achieve your goals. Of course, investment rebalancing does not guarantee a profit or protect against loss in a declining market.

A negative factor to consider when rebalancing with a stock or mutual fund portfolio (that is not invested in a tax-deferred retirement account) is that these transactions could generate capital gains and losses when these funds are bought or sold. These sales and purchases could become taxable events. I tell my clients that sometimes it's better to pay the tax and keep their gains, instead of watching their account balance go up and down.

DOLLAR COST AVERAGING

Dollar cost averaging is a systematic way of saving for the long run. Women have been using this concept for years. Let's just say you love to shop. The shoes you have been looking for are on sale. The price before the sale was $100. However, you can get them today for $50. This is a great deal. You can now buy two pairs of shoes for $100, instead of just one.

This concept can also be applied with investing. If you were buying a hypothetical stock for $100 and the price fell to $50, most people would get discouraged and feel like they were losing money if they already owned the stock. However, the person that understands long-term investing might see this as an opportunity to buy more for less. In this case, because of its current market price you can buy two shares of stock for $100, compared to buying just one share for $100. I see this problem all the time, when individuals invest in their company's retirement plan. They stop their contributions to their retirement plan when the market is doing poorly; just when this could be the best time to buy more shares because the prices are lower.

It's important to understand that dollar-cost averaging does not assure a profit or protect against loss in declining markets. To be effective, there must be a continuous investment regardless of price fluctuations. Investors should consider their financial ability to continue to make purchases through periods of low price levels.

Real Estate

Real estate is an area where some people choose to invest. For some individuals buying a home will be a way to build assets. Instead of renting, you are in a position where you can take advantage of the equity that accumulates in the value of your property over time. Others buy real estate as an investment. Rental property can provide a steady stream of income during retirement.

There are advantages and disadvantages for investing in rental property. One advantage of investing in rental property is this is a way to earn additional income. Another advantage for investing in rental property is that the value of the property increases over time. The property can later be sold to provide additional revenue to support your retirement.

Rental property also has its disadvantages. The wrong tenant in the property could cost you a lot of money. If they don't pay the rent, you could find yourself paying for their living expenses. Sometimes it takes several months to get a tenant removed from a property. I have seen cases where individuals who own several rental properties are not making money. Some of their properties are making a profit while others are losing money. Owners should look at their properties as an investment. Rental property owners should establish expected rates of return for each property separately from each other. This makes it easier to determine which property they should keep and which property should be sold.

One key element to successful investing is to stick to your long-term objective. For example, if it is retirement for you and college funding for your children, you should have separate investment strategies in place at the same time for both objectives.

Summary for Investing

- Seek the opinions of others who are knowledgeable in the area in which you are considering.
- Separate your investments into short-term and long-term time horizons.
- Match investments to your time horizons.
- For periods of time longer than two years, consider equity investments which can help the investor keep pace with taxes and inflation over the long term.
- Make sure that your equity portfolio is diversified (funds invested in a variety of equity investments that tend to react differently to market movement).
- Determine for yourself, based on your financial situation, your tolerance for risk, and your time horizon, when the time is right to buy or sell a stock or mutual fund.
- Automatic rebalancing takes emotion out of the decision-making process of buying and selling stocks or mutual funds.
- Real estate can be another way to grow your assets.

In the next chapter, let's see how investing can have a tremendous impact on your retirement.

CHAPTER 8

Your Ideal Retirement

FOR most people, planning for retirement is a first-time event. Whenever we do something for the first time we may be a little nervous. This is normal; don't let the fear of the unknown prevent you from taking the steps necessary to plan for your retirement. As I mentioned before, retirement is like a long vacation. Why don't we create an ideal vacation, and then transfer this concept into your ideal retirement.

START PLANNING EARLY

Let's say you wanted to take your family on a week vacation in June to the Bahamas. You've heard from several friends that Atlantis at Paradise Island in the Bahamas is a great place. Would you wait a week before the trip to book your hotel and your airline ticket? Would you wait a week before the trip to find out if you and your wife can take the time off from work? The kids went online to the Atlantis website. They saw pictures of the waterslides and are looking forward to having a good time. Your wife also went online and is looking forward to enjoying a romantic dinner at the restaurant overlooking the aquarium.

At the last minute, you're able to put the vacation together. The hotel has rooms available, and the airline also has seats available. There is only one problem—because you waited until the last minute, the trip is going to cost more than you can afford. Can you imagine the look on your wife's and kids' faces when you tell them the family can't afford to go? Instead of having fun in the sun, you now have a doom and gloom experience. Your ideal vacation didn't necessarily have to turn out this way. It could have been better if you had only done a little planning. This is also true with your retirement. The sooner you start planning, the more options you'll have toward meeting your goals.

Establish a Specific Retirement Date

A common problem I see in the area of retirement planning is that most people don't have a specific retirement date in mind and fail to start saving early. For example, you may want to retire between age 60 and 65. When you start with a range of ages, it doesn't create a sense of urgency. A range of ages creates a feeling that you have time and encourages you to procrastinate in saving for your retirement. If you select a specific age instead of a range of ages, it makes the goal more definable. By having a specific date, you'll be motivated to take action and make your retirement a reality. There's a big difference in the amount of money you will need if you start your retirement at age 60 instead of age 65. If you retire at age 60, this means you are starting to spend your retirement assets five years earlier, compared to retiring at age 65. Retiring at age 65 gives you five additional years of income from employment and might provide the income to save more or pay off debts.

Some People Retire Too Soon

The other problem I have found in this area occurs when individuals retire at the age that they become eligible to retire. Just because you are eligible based on age doesn't mean you are financially able to retire. I run into this problem all the time. Some individuals retire because they reached retirement eligible age, and immediately after retirement, they realize they don't have enough income to meet their retirement needs. They have given up good jobs with benefits, such as medical insurance and vacation time, only to have to go back into the work force, taking jobs with less pay and perhaps no benefits. Typically, I have found that most individuals have some savings for retirement, but they don't get serious about how much income they'll need on a monthly basis for retirement until about two to three years before their retirement date. This process of calculating how much income you will need during retirement should start at least 10 to 15 years before retirement, if not sooner.

Failure to Account for Income Taxes

Another area that is often overlooked in calculating retirement needs is income tax. Many people fail to account for income taxes that could reduce their income by 15 percent to 20 percent. Just because you are retired doesn't mean that your favorite uncle, Uncle Sam (the United States government), goes away. Pension income is simply a paycheck you receive during retirement. While you are working, your employer typically withholds federal income tax when you get paid. The same process applies in retirement. Income taxes should be deducted when the income is distributed to you, or you may have to pay penalty and interest fees in addition to the income taxes that were due for the underpayment of your taxes. Often your income needs drop during retirement, but not enough to take you to a lower income tax bracket. Some individuals may actually remain in the same tax bracket in retirement they had during their working years.

How Long Should Your Money Last?

An additional retirement oversight individuals make is that they don't consider how long their money should last. A good indicator of how long you might live is how long your parents, grandparents, aunts, and uncles have lived. Today, with medical technology, you might consider even adding to that average. For many married couples, it is possible that one or both of them might live beyond the age of 90. If you were considering retiring at age 60, your retirement income may need to last another 30 years.

WHAT IS YOUR DESIRED RETIREMENT LIFESTYLE?

Another factor you should take into consideration is the type of lifestyle you want to have when you retire. How active you are now will give you an idea of how much money you will need in retirement. Retirement is like a permanent vacation; when you are on vacation, you spend more money on leisure activities. During retirement, you will have more time to do the things you couldn't do before. It's quite possible that some individuals will need just as much income to maintain their quality of life in retirement as they did before retirement.

UNDERSTANDING WHAT YOUR PENSION AND SOCIAL SECURITY WILL PAY

Some people believe that the income received from their company pension and Social Security will be sufficient to take care of them during retirement. One question I pose to clients is, "Would you be able to take a fairly substantial pay cut today and maintain your quality of life?" Most often, the reply is no. The reality is that the income received in retirement from your pension and Social Security could be considerably less than your current income. If you need additional income and didn't save enough along the way, financially you may not be able to live your life the way you want to.

School teachers who work 10 months out of the year understand this process. They get the benefit of spending time with their families during the summer months, but they don't get paid for two months. Many of them take only a portion of their normal income during the 10 months they work and use the difference to provide income for the two months they don't work. There are two ways of doing this. They either save a portion of their pay, or they have their employer put aside a portion of their income and pay them the difference during those two months.

Retirement is similar to a long summer vacation. If the income from your pension and Social Security isn't enough to maintain your quality of life, the difference will have to be made up from your personal savings and investments. If your savings and investments are not enough to maintain your quality of life during retirement, then you may have to consider working a little longer in your current position or consider working part-time during retirement to supplement your income.

What Rate of Return
Is Needed During Retirement?

This leads me to another common mistake found in retirement planning. Many people don't know what rate of return on their funds they'll need to achieve so that they won't run out of money during their retirement. They may not reach their retirement goal for one of two main reasons. One, they invest their funds too conservatively and don't make sufficient gains. Two, they invest too aggressively and expose their funds to too much risk and lose money. Wouldn't it be a great idea to calculate how much money you'll need and invest at a comfortable rate toward potentially reaching your goal? The answer, of course, is yes.

One strategy for addressing this problem is investing your funds in a diversified portfolio. A properly diversified portfolio can be key to growing and maintaining the appropriate amount of income during retirement. For example, I once met with two employees who worked for a major company. Both held the same position and had worked for the company for 30 years. They contributed approximately the same amount of funds into their company's retirement plan and were eligible for retirement. One of the two employees was not comfortable in investing in the stock market and invested 100 percent of her contributions in an account that provided a fixed interest rate. During the 30-year period, this employee accumulated $100,000 in retirement fund. The other associate's contributions were diversified among market-sensitive investments, and she accumulated considerably more during the same time. Of course, investments are subject to market risk, will fluctuate and may lose value, and each investor should decide how to allocate his or her retirement funds based on their own particular set of circumstances and individual tolerance for risk. In this example, if both employees require a similar amount of income to maintain their quality of life, it goes without saying that the employee with more money accumulated will have more options. While this example is intended to illustrate how taking on more investment risk can bring with it the potential for greater return over the long term, it is not indicative of the performance of any particular investment or financial product, and individual results can vary widely.

SUMMARY FOR PLANNING YOUR IDEAL RETIREMENT

- Start planning early.
- Establish a specific retirement date.
- Understand that just because you are eligible based on age doesn't mean you are financially ready to retire.
- Take into consideration that during retirement income taxes could reduce income by 15 percent to 20 percent.
- Consider your life expectancy when determining the amount of funds you will need.
- A factor you should take into consideration is the type of lifestyle you want to have when you retire.

- Understanding what your pension plan or social security will pay.
- Determine the rate of return needed during retirement.

With your increased knowledge and understanding regarding your retirement planning, let's review ways, in the next chapter, to implement these concepts.

CHAPTER 9

It's Your Move

WHAT'S your next move? I've been fortunate to live in the world of both the haves and the have-nots (People who have money and the people who don't). I was motivated by hundreds of people across this country who have been asking the question, "Where can I go to get the information so that I am no longer financially illiterate?" I was inspired by two people in 2008 to start this journey in writing this book. One was Sarano Kelley, my life coach. I played his game, "Win Your Life in 90 Days," in which he challenged me with the following:

If you were to die in 90 days, is there something you would have regretted? If you had a second chance, what would you do differently?

In that "90 days" game I wanted to achieve four things:

1. Improve my spirituality by getting closer to God. The daily Bible reading has enhanced my life tremendously.
2. Have a closer relationship with my wife and children. I now have date nights with my life partner of 28 years, and our relationship has never been closer. One of the greatest joys that have come out of the game is spending more time with my daughter Jasmin and my son Gerald III. They both have made my wife and me proud by growing up to be outstanding individuals.

3. Get physically fit. I have learned how to take care of the one body our Lord has blessed me with. I have learned how to eat right and exercise. My spinning class at 5:45 a.m. on Wednesday morning at LA Fitness has been the glue that has been there during my transformation.
4. Help others gain financial understanding. The most difficult challenge during those 90 days was writing this book.

Before meeting Sarano Kelley, I only read books for school and work. Now I read because I love to. Of the books that I have read, one that has had a major impact on my financial understanding is *The Richest Man in Babylon,* by George S. Clason. Since reading it, I have given away over 500 copies of this book. I heard about it at age 52, while attending an insurance conference in Florida. It is amazing how the right people come into your life at the right time.

The speaker, another life coach named Bryan Dodge, cited the book as one of the greatest he has ever read on becoming wealthy. He challenged everyone in the room who had not read the book to do so. I was inspired by him and bought the book that same week. It made such a great impression on me that I bought copies for each of my children and gave them a challenge. I wanted them to read this book in one week, and then write an essay as to how they would implement these concepts into their lives. If they were able to accomplish this task, I would give each of them $100.00.

The results were amazing. I have never seen them so focused in their lives. When I came home, instead of watching television or playing games, they were reading. The most wonderful thing about this experience is seeing, one year later, how these principles are being utilized in their lives. I have seen my daughter, who would spend every dime she would get on clothing and shoes, turn into someone who wants to invest her extra funds in stocks. I have seen my son, who wanted to be involved in multiple sports and social activities, become the president of two organizations while maintaining straight 'A's" and making the principal's honor role for two semesters during his senior year in high school. Looking back at the results, it is the best two hundred dollars I have ever spent.

For those of you reading this book, if it touches your heart, I want you to do something that comes from one of my favorite artists, Diana Ross: "...reach out and touch somebody's hand and make this world a better place if you can." If this book moves you, I want you to buy five copies of this book and share them with the most important people in your life. If they are unable to read it, read it to them. When my grandmother was old and had difficulty seeing, she would ask me to read the *Bible* to her. As I read and was having some difficulty pronouncing some of the words, she would say them for me. It was not until many years later that I realized what she was doing. She did not need me to read the *Bible* to her; she knew the words even before I could say them. It was her way of encouraging me as a child to get to know our Lord and Savior Jesus Christ. During those times, I would get closer to my grandmother. It was wonderful to see how her values have transformed the lives of our entire family.

For my family and me, the gift of education has been the ticket out of poverty. I know what it is like to be poor. I'm the youngest of four children. I grew up in Jamaica, where we did not have an electric water heater; we had solar water heating. My parents would take their showers first, and then my sisters and brother. By the time it was my turn the water was always cold.

I remember growing up in Liberty City in Miami. When I got my first job, I had to walk five miles to work and five miles back home every day. I couldn't depend on the bus, because the system was unreliable and I had to get to work on time. I can still remember my joy when I was able to save $600 to buy my brother's old car, so that I had transportation to drive to school when I started college.

This book, for many people, is the ticket out of poverty. I can remember my grandmother saying, "I can give you food for today, but if I teach you how to fish you can feed your family forever." I hope this book will be a blessing to you and your families, and that you can be a blessing to others by sharing this gift.

To God Be the Glory

In my second book, I will share the blessing of having insurance to protect your family. In my third book, I will share some lessons on how to pass on your wealth to your children, your grandchildren, and for generations to come.

About the Author

GERALD C. GRANT, Jr., MBA
Branch Director of Financial Planning
AXA Advisors' South Florida Branch

THE author brought to AXA Advisors, LLC over eleven years of banking experience and was previously associated with Citibank, where he held the position of Branch Vice President and Cluster Manager. Prior to Citibank, Gerald was a Branch Manager with Great Western Bank. While at Great Western, he was "Branch Manager of the Year" for two consecutive years. In 1991, Gerald was named "Banker of the Year" by the Miami-Dade Urban Bankers Association. His experience and knowledge are now used to help clients focus on estate planning*, wealth accumulation and protection, life insurance, retirement planning* and other financial services and products.

He is an active member of the South Florida community, serving on the foundation board of directors for Florida International University (FIU) and Florida A & M University (FAMU).

Gerald is a past president of the FIU Alumni Association and served on the United Way Resource Management Committee. He is also a member of the Orange Bowl Committee, the 100 Black Men of South Florida and a member of Phi Beta Sigma Fraternity, Inc. Theta Rho Sigma Chapter. Gerald is a past-president of (NAIFA) National Association of Insurance and Financial Advisors, Miami-Dade Chapter. In 2005, AXA Advisors honored

Gerald by naming him the "Regional Honor Associate" for the company's Southern Division, and in 1999 he was the recipient of the Community Service Award for AXA Advisor's Miami/Ft. Lauderdale Branch.

Gerald holds an A.A. degree from Miami-Dade College and both Bachelors' and Master's degrees in Business Administration from FIU. He also holds FINRA Series 7, 24, 63 and 65 securities registrations.

Gerald lives in Palmetto Bay with his wife, Jennifer and their two children, Jasmin and Gerald III.

*Using life insurance and other financial products

Gerald Grant, Jr. is a registered representative and investment advisor representative who offers securities products and investment advisory services through AXA Advisors, LLC (212-314-4600), member FINRA/SIPC, and is an agent who offers annuity and insurance products through AXA Network, LLC and/or its insurance agency affiliates. CA Insurance License #: 0D09274. AXA Network does business in California as AXA Network Insurance Agency of California, LLC. Individuals may transact business and/or respond to inquiries only in state(s) in which they are properly licensed and registered. AXA Advisors and it affiliates and associates do not provide tax or legal advice. This book is for informational purposes only and is not intended as legal, tax or investment advice. Please consult your tax and/or legal and other professional advisors regarding your particular circumstances. PPG-52125(10/09)

SERVICES AVAILABLE

Gerald Grant, Jr. is available to make presentations
at national conferences, conduct seminars, and speak to
business organizations, universities, church groups and
people in business.

For more information about Gerald Grant, Jr.
as a Financial Professional of AXA Advisors, LLC,
you can call him at his office at (305) 670-4679,
on his cell phone at (786) 459-8282,
or you can visit his website:
www.GeraldGrantJr.**MyAXA-ADVISORS**.com

You can obtain information about ordering this book at:
www.GeraldGrantJr.com

or by writing to Gerald Grant, Jr. at:
P.O. Box 566567
Miami, FL 33256-6567

INDEX